Governing *the* Golden State

Elizabeth Anderson Lopez

Consultants

Kristina Jovin, M.A.T.
Alvord Unified School District
Teacher of the Year

Vanessa Ann Gunther, Ph.D.
Department of History
Chapman University

Publishing Credits

Rachelle Cracchiolo, M.S.Ed., *Publisher*
Conni Medina, M.A.Ed., *Managing Editor*
Emily R. Smith, M.A.Ed., *Series Developer*
June Kikuchi, *Content Director*
Marc Pioch, M.A.Ed., and Susan Daddis, M.A.Ed., *Editors*
Courtney Roberson, *Senior Graphic Designer*

Image Credits: Cover and p.1 (foreground) eye35 stock/Alamy Stock Photo, (background) AP Photo/Rich Pedroncelli; p.4 Library of Congress [LC-USZ62-13037]; p.5 Bill Clark/CQ Roll Call/Getty Images; pp.6–7 United States Capitol; pp.10–11 National Archives and Records Administration [1667751]; pp.11, 32, back cover Courtesy of the California History Room, California State Library, Sacramento, California; p.12 (inset) Al Seib/Los Angeles Times via Getty Images; pp.12–13 Creative Commons Attribution-ShareAlike 4.0 International by Carole J. Buckwalter; p.13 (top) Library of Congress [LC-USZ62-41653]; p.14 (bottom) Ted Soqui/Corbis via Getty Images; p.15 (top) George Rose/Getty Images, (full page) Trinity Mirror/Mirrorpix/Alamy Stock Photo; p.16 (bottom) Ron Riesterer/Oakland Tribune Staff Archives, (inset seal) United States Department of Justice; pp.16–17 Library of Congress [LC-DIG-highsm-10515]; p.17 (top) Los Angeles Times Photographic Archive. Department of Special Collections, Charles E. Young Research Library, UCLA; pp.20–21 Glenn Koenig/Los Angeles Times via Getty Images; p.21 (top) State of California Department of Justice; p.22 Michael Dwyer/Alamy Stock Photo; p.23 Saul Martinez/Reuters; pp.24–25 Lucy Nicholson/Reuters; p.24 (inset) s_bukley/Shutterstock.com; p.26 (top) Khalid Al-Mousily/Reuters/Newscom; p.27 (bottom) United States Congress, US Senate Photo by Becky Hammel; p.31 George Rose/Getty Images; all other images from iStock and/or Shutterstock.

Library of Congress Cataloging-in-Publication Data
Names: Lopez, Elizabeth Anderson, author.
Title: Governing the golden state / Elizabeth Anderson Lopez.
Description: Huntington Beach, CA : Teacher Created Materials, Inc., [2018] | Includes index.
Identifiers: LCCN 2017014173 (print) | LCCN 2017031126 (ebook) | ISBN 9781425855000 (eBook) | ISBN 9781425832483 (pbk.)
Subjects: LCSH: California--Politics and government.
Classification: LCC JK8716 (ebook) | LCC JK8716 .L66 2018 (print) | DDC 320.4794--dc23
LC record available at https://lccn.loc.gov/2017014173

Teacher Created Materials
5301 Oceanus Drive
Huntington Beach, CA 92649-1030
http://www.tcmpub.com
ISBN 978-1-4258-3248-3

Printed in China
Nordica.012019.CA21801586

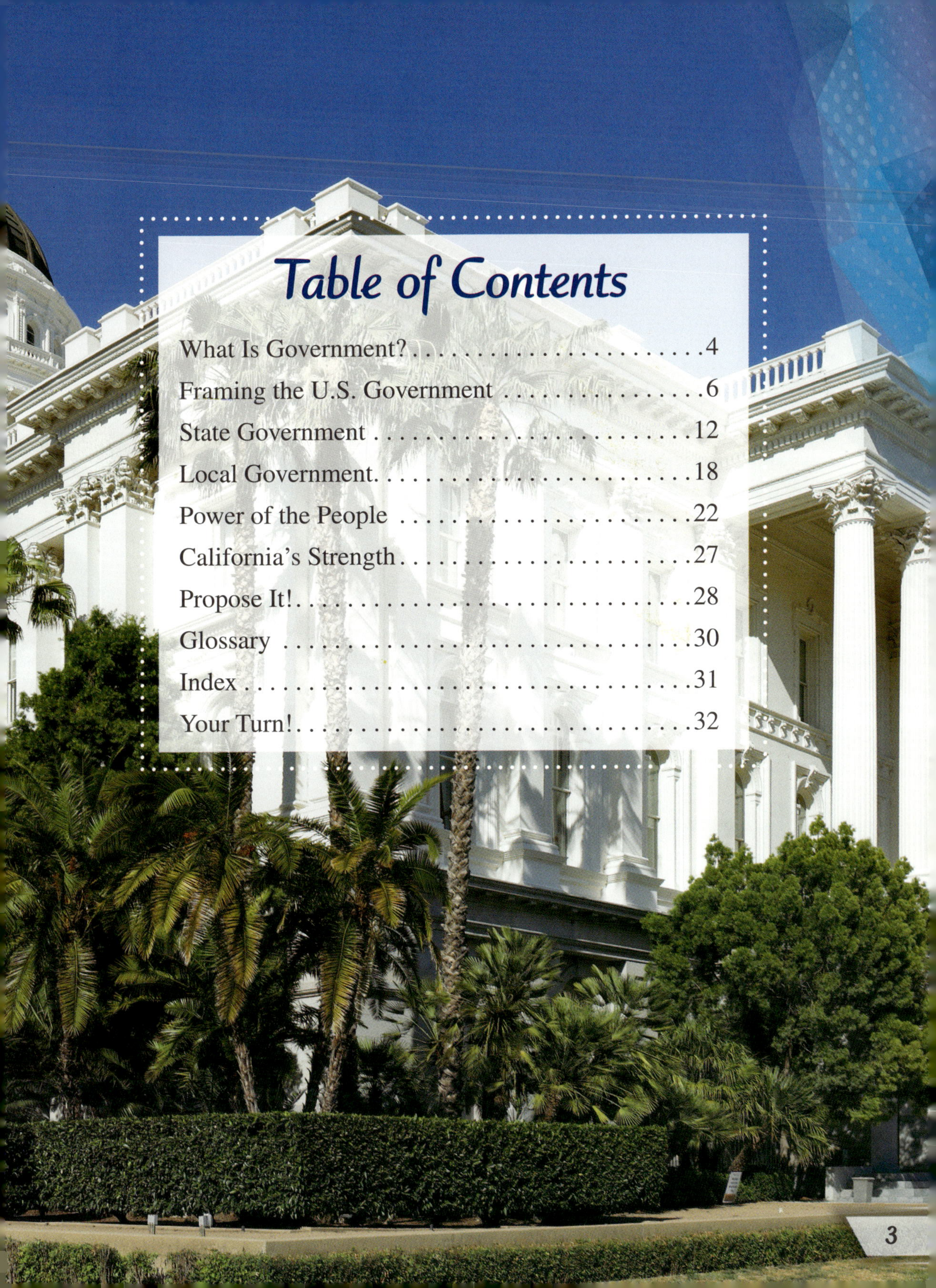

Table of Contents

What Is Government?

Government is a system of rules and laws. It also includes the people who make, **enforce**, and interpret those laws. It has many levels. The federal government rules the whole country. California has its own state government. It is modeled after the federal level. Within states, there are counties and cities. These smaller areas also have laws and leaders.

By voting, all citizens can help improve the way their cities, states, and even the country are run. They can pick the leaders they want. They can vote for or against laws. People should speak up when they are happy or unhappy with what elected leaders at all levels are doing. Why? Because government leaders work for the people.

Running for President

There are three requirements to run for president.

1. The candidate must be at least 35 years old.
2. The candidate must be a natural-born citizen of the United States.
3. The candidate must have lived in the United States for at least 14 years.

Civics

Richard Nixon was the first president born in California.

President Barack Obama gives a speech to Congress.

Framing the U.S. Government

In 1787, the United States was still a young country. Its original government was not working. Something had to be done. A group of **delegates** met in Philadelphia to fix the problem. These men were called the *framers*. They set up the plan for the new government. The plan they came up with was the U.S. Constitution.

Not everyone in the country agreed with this bold, new plan. They thought the new government would have too much power. They felt their rights might be taken away. So, the Bill of Rights was added. These first 10 **amendments** protect the rights of the people. The Bill of Rights became part of the Constitution in 1791.

Congress OF THE United States
begun and held at the City of New-York, on
Wednesday the Fourth of March, one thousand seven hundred and eighty nine

The Bill of Rights

On September 17, 1787, the U.S. Constitution was signed.

Hamilton's Mistake

There are some errors in the Constitution. Alexander Hamilton was one of the delegates. He took charge of the signing process. He wrote the names of the states next to each signer's name. Next to Benjamin Franklin, he misspelled Pennsylvania as "Pensylvania."

The Three Branches

The framers didn't want one person or group to have too much power. That's why they split the federal government into three branches. The branches are legislative, executive, and judicial. Each group has a different job. The legislative branch makes the laws. The executive branch enforces the laws. The judicial branch interprets the laws.

The leaders of the three branches work together. They make sure the other groups are doing their jobs. This system is called **checks and balances**. Congress is the legislative branch. The Senate and House of Representatives make the laws. The president runs the executive branch and makes sure the laws are followed. The Supreme Court is the judicial branch. The **justices** who sit on this court make sure the laws are fair.

Executive Branch

The president, vice president and cabinet enforce laws.

Legislative Branch

Congress, which is made up of the House of Representatives and Senate, makes laws.

Judicial Branch

The U.S. Supreme Court interprets laws.

U.S. and State Constitutions

The Constitution is the **blueprint** for how to rule the United States. It is also the supreme law of the land. This means that all federal laws overrule state laws. Each state has its own constitution, too. That is the plan for how to run the state. California's was approved in 1849 before it became a state.

State and federal constitutions have some things in common. They outline how the government will be structured. They each have a **preamble**, articles, and sections. And they each have a bill of rights.

However, there are some things that are different. The laws in state constitutions deal with state issues. It is easier to change state constitutions. California's state constitution has been revised more than five hundred times!

And the Winner Is...Federal!

The framers of the Constitution knew there might be clashes between the federal and state governments. So, they tried to solve problems when they could. Article VI, Section 2 is known as the *Supremacy Clause*. It says that states will not interfere with federal matters. The clause also notes that federal laws overrule all state laws.

Civics

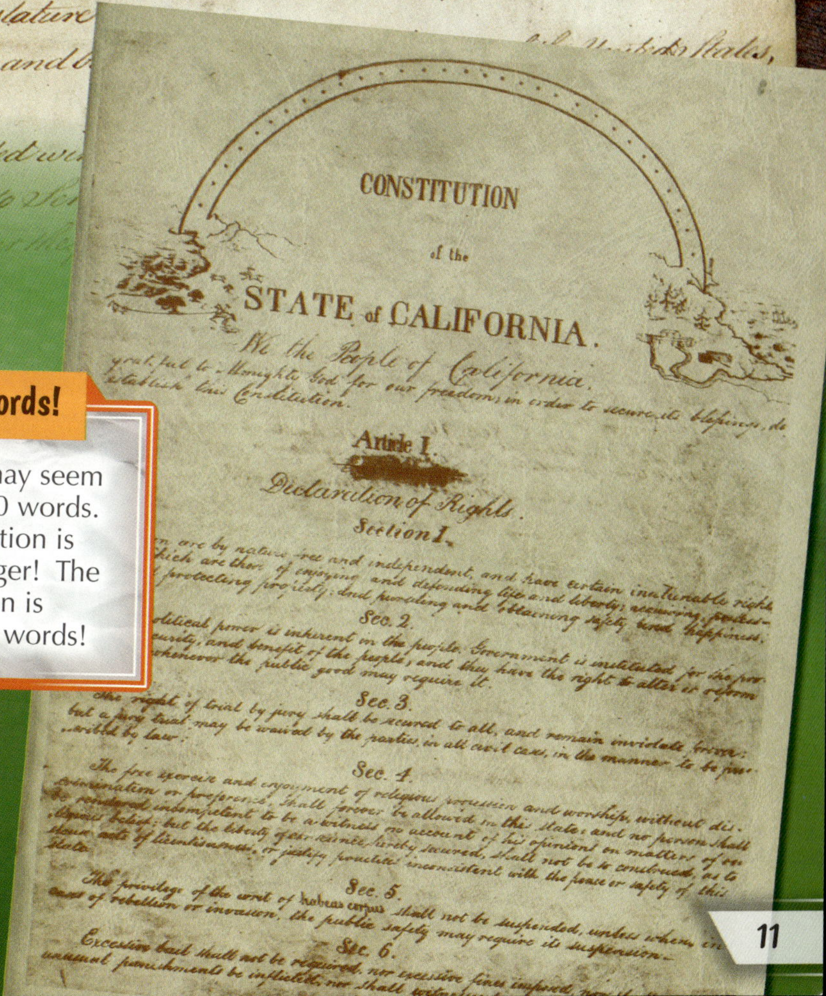

That's a Lot of Words!

The U.S. Constitution may seem long. It has about 4,500 words. But California's constitution is more than 15 times longer! The shortest state constitution is Vermont's. It has 8,295 words!

State Government

California has the same structure as the federal government. It uses the same checks and balances. The state legislative branch makes laws. The executive branch of the state enforces these laws. And the state's judicial branch interprets the laws. These three groups work with each other to decide how to run things in the state.

Legislative Branch

California's legislative branch has two parts. The state assembly has 80 members. Each member is elected for a two-year term. The state senate has 40 members. They are elected for four-year terms. People in the assembly and senate are elected based on the **districts** where they live. They make state laws. They also approve the state budget.

Sheila James Kuehl

In 1994, Sheila James Kuehl became the first openly gay person elected to the California State Assembly. Six years later, Kuehl was elected to the state senate. By 2007, she had written 171 **bills** that were signed into laws.

Earl Warren

Earl Warren was born and raised in California. In 1914, he earned a law degree from the University of California, Berkeley. Three years later, he joined the army. After that, Warren spent most of his life in politics. He served as California's governor for 10 years. In his third term, he was appointed as the chief justice of the U.S. Supreme Court. He held that role for 16 years.

California senate chambers

Executive Branch

The state's executive branch is set up like the federal one. The governor leads the state for a four-year term. His or her job is to enforce state laws and to control the state budget. The governor makes sure the state is ready in case of an emergency.

This branch includes other people, too. The lieutenant governor is like a vice president. He or she can take the place of the governor, if needed. The attorney general is the state's lawyer. The secretary of state manages the elections. The state treasurer is the state's top banker. They all help run the state.

Cruz M. Bustamante

Cruz M. Bustamante first ran for public office in 1993. He was elected to the state assembly. In 1999, he became the lieutenant governor of California for eight years. He was the first Latino to serve in a state office in more than a century. While there, Bustamante focused on school issues that would help students of all ages.

March Fong Eu

In 1966, March Fong Eu was California's first Asian American woman in the state assembly. Eu fought to save the environment. She also worked on laws that dealt with women's rights. In 1974, she was elected to be secretary of state. She was the first Asian American to hold that post.

Ronald Reagan served two terms as California's govenor.

Judicial Branch

The state's judicial branch interprets laws. This branch is made up of the state's court system. The California court system is the largest in the nation.

The 58 superior courts are the trial courts. This is where cases are heard. People's guilt or innocence is decided. **Civil** cases also take place in superior courts. If people are unhappy with a decision, they can bring the case to a court of appeal. There are six district courts of appeal. The appeals courts review decisions made by lower courts. They make sure all laws were followed in each case.

The highest **appellate** court in the state is the supreme court. There, justices review judgments made by the courts of appeal. Most of the time, the state supreme court has the power to decide which cases it will look at. It is similar to the U.S. Supreme Court, the highest court in the country.

Wiley W. Manuel

In 1953, Wiley W. Manuel began working for the attorney general's office. He worked there for 23 years until he was appointed to the state supreme court. Manuel was the first African American named to the court. He said that success came to him because he "worked hard," which "was the only way a kid like me was going to make it."

U.S. Court of Appeals in San Francisco

Rose Elizabeth Bird

Rose Elizabeth Bird was appointed to the California supreme court in 1977. She served for 10 years. Bird was the first woman to serve on the court. She was also the first woman to be chief justice. Before that, Bird was the first woman appointed to a cabinet position in the state. She was appointed secretary of agriculture in 1974.

Local Government

There is a third level of government. The local level includes county and city governments. *Counties* are large governed areas in a state. Boards of supervisors run the counties in California. Board members serve four-year terms.

Counties do not have their own laws. The boards enforce state and federal laws. They record **deeds** and permits of land. They issue marriage licenses. The boards make sure roads are built and repaired. County boards are also in charge of elections.

One city in each county is the *county seat.* This is where county offices and courts are located. Other people who help run counties include sheriffs, judges, and **clerks.**

Rancherias

Around the United States, American Indians were forced to live on **reservations.** In California, some of them now live in places called *rancherias*. There are about 100 rancherias in the state. Most California tribes are small. They have systems in place to govern. These include tribal courts and police.

Civics

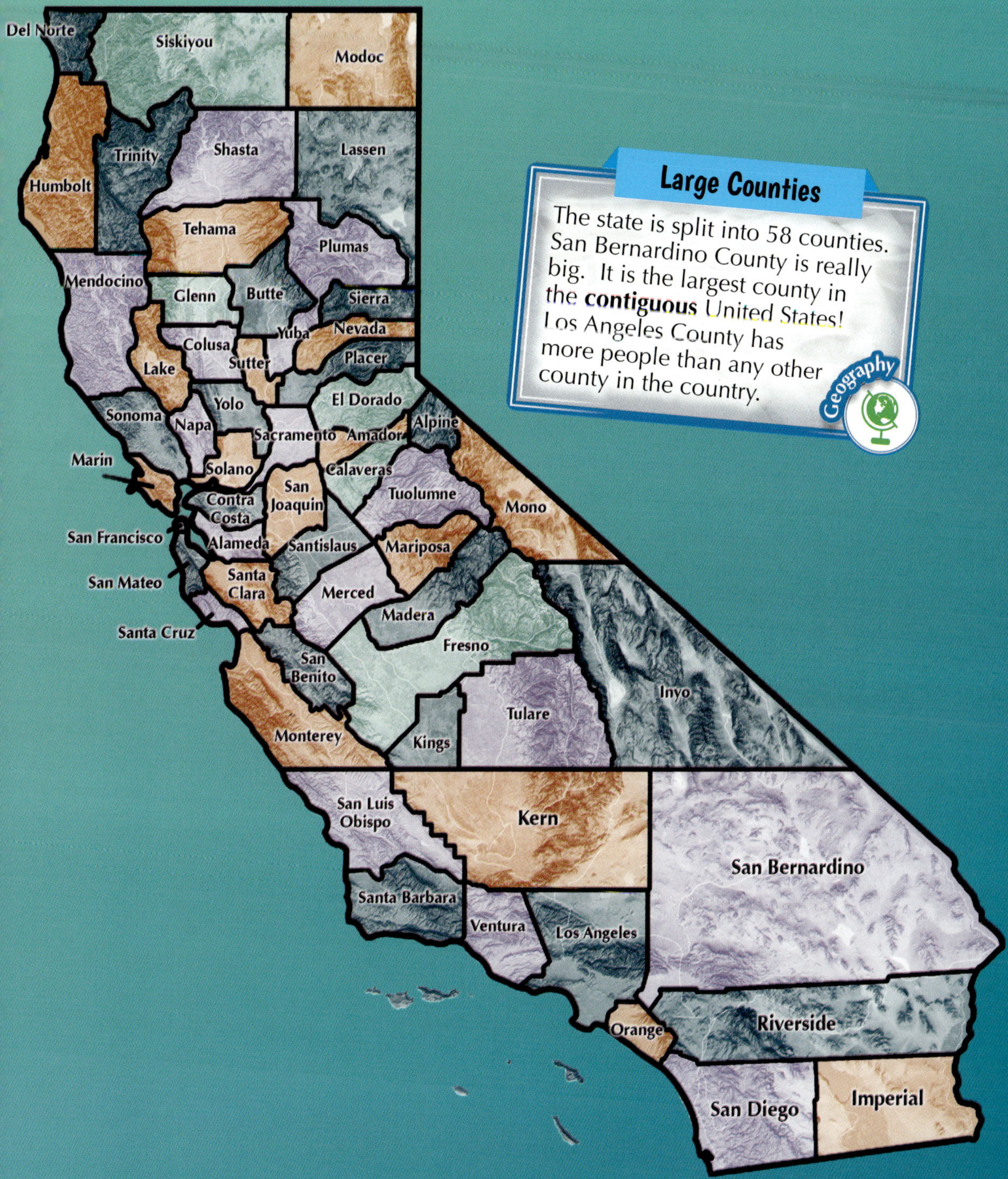

Large Counties

The state is split into 58 counties. San Bernardino County is really big. It is the largest county in the **contiguous** United States! Los Angeles County has more people than any other county in the country.

Geography

People in each city elect a mayor and a city council. These leaders work together. They keep the city safe and clean. Residents have more contact with local leaders than state or federal leaders. That is because city leaders deal with the things that affect people's daily lives. Cities take care of schools, parks, and libraries. The police and fire departments are run at the city level. Water service and trash pickup fall under the control of city leadership, too.

Another part of local government is the school board. A local school board is in charge of public schools. School board members can be elected or appointed. Serving on a school board is a way to serve the community.

Leaders at all three levels of government serve the people. The three levels have some things in common. They all collect taxes. They also make and enforce laws. They work hard to make lives better.

Who Makes the Money?

There are some things that don't apply to all levels. For example, only the federal government prints money. All the paper money in the country is made in Washington, DC and Texas at the Bureau of Engraving and Printing plants. Coins are made at four of the six U.S. Mint sites.

Economics

Kamala Harris

Kamala Harris began her career as a lawyer. In 2003, Harris ran for district attorney of San Francisco. She became the first woman to hold the office. Harris served in her post for six years. After that, she won the election for attorney general. Harris was the first woman to serve there, too. She used the things she learned in San Francisco to help the state grow. Harris was elected to the U.S. Senate in 2016.

Many city council meetings are open to the public.

Power of the People

Citizens can play an active role in government. They don't have to run for office. But they can vote and work with leaders to make change.

Voting

People vote for leaders at all three levels of government. They can also help make laws in their counties and cities. If someone has an idea for a new law, they can create a **petition**. A certain number of people must sign it to get to the next step. If they succeed, it can be on a ballot, and citizens can vote on it. This is called an *initiative*. People also vote on referendums. These approve or change current laws.

When people first run for office, they often do it at the local level. They feel they can make an impact in their communities by being part of the governing bodies.

Are You Qualified?

To vote in California, people must meet certain requirements. They must be U.S. citizens and live in the state. They also must be at least 18 years old on Election Day. There are three ways to register. They can go online or mail in their paperwork. The third option is to go to their local Department of Motor Vehicles (DMV).

Your Voice Matters

One of California's recent initiatives was Proposition 67. People voted to ban plastic bags that are only used one time. This ban mostly affects grocery stores. Many people bring reusable bags when they shop.

Civics

Removal from Office

When people vote, they vote for the person they think will do the best job. But what if an elected official fails at the job? Do these people get to stay in their jobs until their terms are over? In California, a leader can be fired, or **recalled**. To remove a person from office, the people must vote on it. Recalls are not common. There have been 32 recall attempts. Only five leaders in the state have ever been recalled.

Federal leaders can also be removed from office, or **impeached**. This is similar to a recall, but the people do not vote on it. Congress is in charge of impeachments. The framers felt leaders must have the **consent of the governed**. That is why they included impeachments in the U.S. Constitution. Like recalls, impeachments are rare. Only 16 federal officials have been impeached.

Governor Gray Davis

Dismissed from Office

The most prominent California politician to be recalled was Governor Gray Davis in 2003. But he wasn't the first. Four other elected state leaders have also been recalled and removed from office:

- 1913: Senator Marshall Black
- 1914: Senator Edwin Grant
- 1994: Assembly Member Paul Horcher
- 1995: Assembly Member Doris Allen

In 2013, people gathered to share their feelings about the recall of Governor Davis.

Edward Royce

Edward Royce was first elected to the House of Representatives in 1992. He continues to serve today. Royce works on many issues affecting the country and the state. One of them is to improve the education system. He is a supporter of Science, Technology, Engineering, and Mathematics (STEM) programs.

U.S. Capitol

California's Strength

California is a huge state. It holds a lot of power. It has the most people and the most districts of any state. The state has 53 districts. Each one elects a person to the U.S. House of Representatives. California also has two U.S. Senators, like all other states. In total, California has 55 members in Congress, the most of any state.

California is also the richest state in the country. Many industries call the state home. From computer and tech companies to farming and movies, California has it all. State and local leaders have important jobs. They must work together to make and enforce laws that help the state succeed.

The people in the state have important jobs, too. They must use their voices to make sure that they have a say in how to keep the state golden.

Dianne Feinstein

Dianne Feinstein is a woman of firsts. She was the first female mayor of San Francisco. In 1992, she became the first woman from California elected to the U.S. Senate. During her time as senator, she has worked on laws to help protect the environment. She also worked hard to keep Americans safe. To do this, Feinstein has been a member of many committees. She was the first woman to head two different senate committees.

Propose It!

The initiative process creates new laws at the local government level. Now, it's your turn. Create an initiative for your school. It could be a recycling program or a push to grow a garden. Or you could organize a clothing drive to help kids in homeless shelters. You could also raise money to donate to local animal shelters. After you pick your project, write a proposal. Gather the number of signatures your teacher recommends. Then, have your classmates vote on your initiative.

Glossary

amendments—changes in the wording or meaning of a law or document

appellate—having the power to review and change the decisions made in court

bills—written descriptions of new laws being proposed

blueprint—a detailed plan used as a guide

checks and balances—a system of government put in place so that no one branch has more power than another

civil—relating to laws about people's rights rather than criminal laws

clerks—people responsible for keeping records of information in government offices

consent of the governed—the idea that a government's authority is dependent on the people accepting that authority

contiguous—the lower 48 states in the United States that touch along boundaries

deeds—legal documents that show who the owner of a building is

delegates—people chosen to speak for a state in making new laws and decisions about that state

districts—smaller areas of a certain region, such as a state

enforce—make people follow laws

impeached—charged a public official in office with a crime

justices—judges on the supreme court of a state or country

petition—a written document that people sign to formally request a change

preamble—the introduction to the U.S. Constitution and other legal documents

recalled—voted to remove an elected official before the term ends

reservations—areas of land in the United States for American Indians to live

Index

Your Turn!

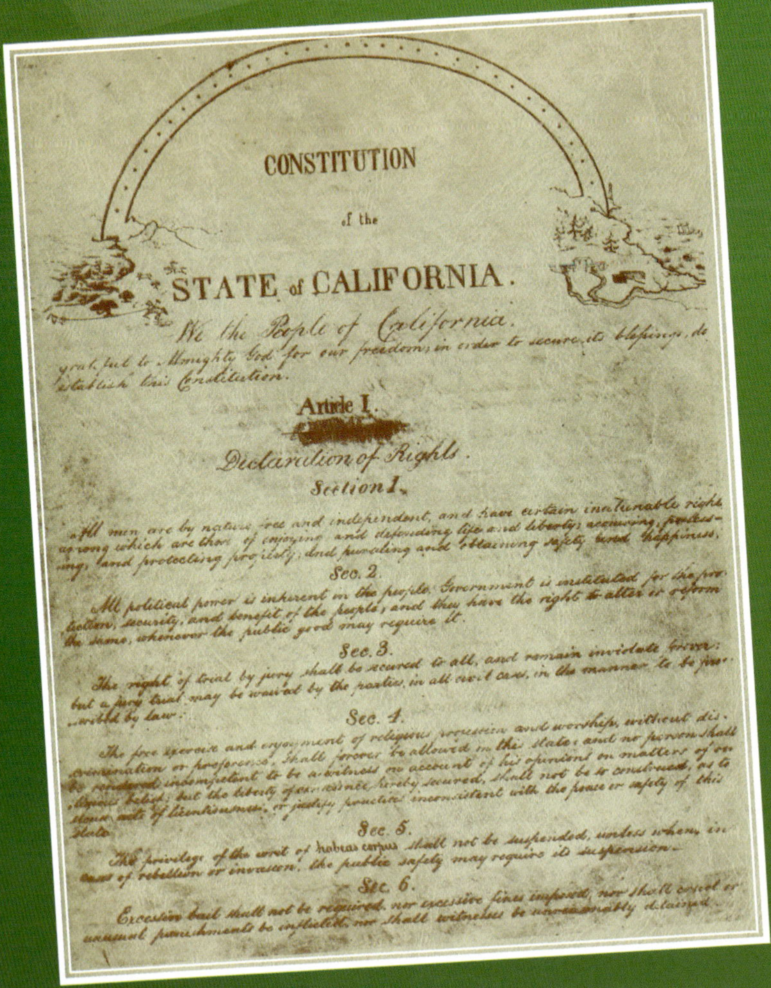

CONSTITUTION

of the

STATE of CALIFORNIA.

We the People of California, grateful to Almighty God for our freedom, in order to secure its blessings, do establish this Constitution.

Article I.

Declaration of Rights.

Section 1.

All men are by nature free and independent, and have certain inalienable rights, among which are those of enjoying and defending life and liberty, acquiring, possessing, and protecting property; and pursuing and obtaining safety and happiness.

Sec. 2.

All political power is inherent in the people. Government is instituted for the protection, security, and benefit of the people; and they have the right to alter or reform the same, whenever the public good may require it.

Sec. 3.

The right of trial by jury shall be secured to all, and remain inviolate forever; but a jury trial may be waived by the parties, in all civil cases, in the manner to be prescribed by law.

Sec. 4.

The free exercise and enjoyment of religious profession and worship, without discrimination or preference, shall forever be allowed in this State; and no person shall be rendered incompetent to be a witness on account of his opinions on matters of religious belief; but the liberty of conscience hereby secured, shall not be so construed, as to excuse acts of licentiousness, or justify practices inconsistent with the peace or safety of this State.

Sec. 5.

The privilege of the writ of habeas corpus shall not be suspended, unless when, in cases of rebellion or invasion, the public safety may require its suspension.

Sec. 6.

Excessive bail shall not be required, nor excessive fines imposed, nor shall cruel or unusual punishments be inflicted, nor shall witnesses be unreasonably detained.

Declaration of Rights

Article I of the Constitution of the State of California includes the Declaration of Rights for its citizens. For example, everyone in the state has the right to speak and write freely. If you were writing a list of rights that all people should have, what would you include? Create your own Declaration of Rights.